For my nieces and nephews: those here now, those yet to be born, and in memory of those who have passed. Your "Unctie" loves you and hopes every page makes you smile. Thank you to the littlest, most fashionable beta reader, Elise DeShields, for affirming my baby steps toward this book.

—EDP

To my Aunt LaVerne, the seamstress of our family

—SW

The illustrations in this book were made with various mixed media and Photoshop. The mixed materials include cardstock, acrylic paints, color pencils, pens, assorted buttons, scraps of fabric, embroidery yarn, and collage magazines, articles, and maps.

Cataloging-in-Publication Data has been applied for and may be obtained from the Library of Congress.

ISBN 978-1-4197-6886-6
eISBN 979-8-88707-053-7

Book design by Heather Kelly and Azalea Afendi

Published in 2026 by Abrams Books for Young Readers, an imprint of ABRAMS.

Printed and bound in China
10 9 8 7 6 5 4 3 2 1

Abrams Books for Young Readers are available at special discounts when purchased in quantity for premiums and promotions as well as fundraising or educational use. Special editions can also be created to specification. For details, contact specialsales@abramsbooks.com or the address below.

ABRAMS is represented in the UK and Europe by Abrams & Chronicle Books, 1 West Smithfield, London EC1A 9JU and Media Participations, 57 rue Gaston Tessier, 75166 Paris, France.
abramsandchronicle.co.uk and media-participations.com info@abramsandchronicle.co.uk

ABRAMS The Art of Books
195 Broadway, New York, NY 10007
abramsbooks.com

CLOTHES TO MAKE YOU SMILE

PATRICK KELLY DESIGNS HIS DREAMS

written by
Eric Darnell Pritchard

illustrated by
Shannon Wright

Abrams Books for Young Readers ♥ New York

When Patrick Kelly was little,
he lost a shirt button.

Buttons cost money, and Patrick's family didn't have a lot. So his grandma, who he called Mama, sewed on whatever button she had.

But the new buttons never matched.
Patrick told Mama he worried other kids
would laugh at the mismatched buttons.

Mama said she would sew on even more buttons, this way the shirt would look so funny that people would not laugh, they would smile. And she was right.

Mama could make you smile
with needle and thread.
Every Sunday, their trip to church
was a fashion parade.

Patrick adored seeing the sea of
gorgeous women in his life—Mama,
his mother (who he called Mother
Dear), aunties, neighbors, and
friends—in all shapes and sizes,
elegantly dressed in skirt suits,
sharp dresses, matching gloves,
and majestic hats.

Patrick thought *when people look good, they feel good.*

No one they knew had much money, so Patrick asked Mama where all the clothes came from.

Mama explained whether clothes, curtains, or quilts—whatever families needed—people made it all themselves.

And they learned how to
make it from their mothers
and their mother's
mothers before them.

Patrick asked so many questions about clothes that Mama brought home old fashion magazines from her job cleaning the houses of wealthy White folks in Vicksburg, Mississippi.

Normally, Patrick didn't like to read, but he lay on Mama's porch for hours leafing through them. Each page was joyful. A world of fabrics, shapes, and colors come alive. It made Patrick feel alive too!

HARPER'S

Patrick never felt this way doing things other boys did, like playing sports with their dads or running around with their friends. Seeing the magazine pages made Patrick smile. So he declared to Mama that he wanted to make clothes like those he saw at church. Then Patrick's clothes could be in the magazines.

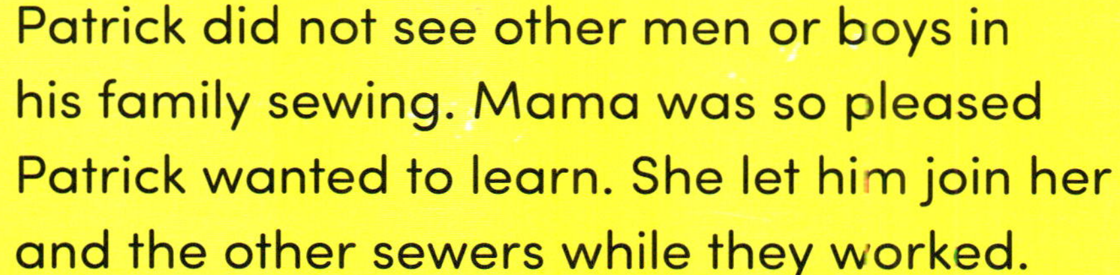

Patrick did not see other men or boys in his family sewing. Mama was so pleased Patrick wanted to learn. She let him join her and the other sewers while they worked.

Mother Dear showed him how to begin . . . with a pencil, paper, and his imagination.

Then Mama and his aunt showed him how to turn his imagination into reality . . . with a needle and thread.

Sewing seemed like magic to Patrick. One minute there would be a pile of material and the next there would be a whole outfit!

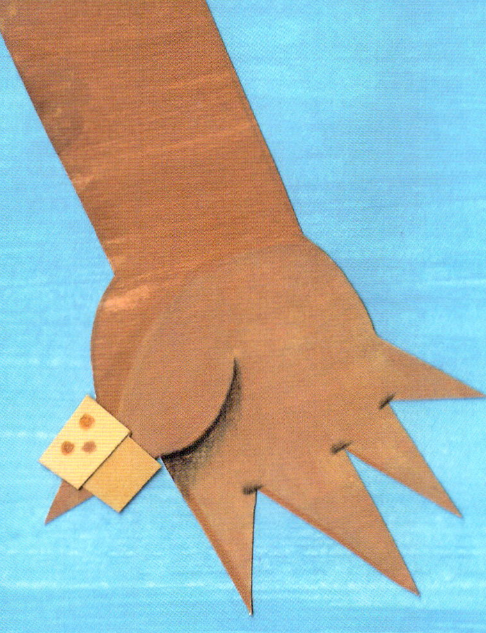

But sewing wasn't as easy as it looked. Needles are sharp.

Ouch!

And getting thread through a needle's eye is hard!

Mama laughed and told Patrick to never give up.

Finally!

Even after that, it wasn't easy.

Everything he made . . .

was a mess.

A hot, hot mess.

Patrick wanted to quit, but Mama and his aunt just laughed some more and told Patrick to have patience. Patrick realized their laughter was the important part.

Their laughter through the hard parts put love in the clothes. So Patrick also learned to laugh and carry on with his work.

By age thirteen, Patrick could dream up, draw, and sew entire outfits. Wild outfits! With tall wigs, huge handbags, and jewelry! His designs became the talk of the town. People asked him to make them outfits for proms, parades, and school plays.

Pretty soon, all of Vicksburg sparkled and shined with people dressed up in Patrick's dreams!

But Vicksburg is a small town. There weren't enough people to wear everything Patrick dreamed up. To get in the fashion magazines, he had to go to the big cities.

Like **Atlanta!**
But store owners
said his designs
were "Too vibrant!"

Like **New York!**
But his teachers said his
designs were "Too tight!"

And **Paris!**
But other designers said
his ideas were "Too tacky!"
"Too much!"

Patrick realized he didn't fit in.
With his Southern accent and coffee-brown skin,
he was different from most fashion folks.

His favorite clothes were different too—overalls with a colorful hat and sneakers. He dressed like a farmer. Everyone else dressed in black, like they were going to a funeral.

Patrick considered giving up and going home.
But he thought *what would Mama do?*
And he laughed and carried on with his work.

He forgot about fitting in with fashion folks. He made coats and sold them on the street.

He cooked big dinners using Mama's old recipes and sold them to make more money to buy fabric.

He made friends with many dancers, singers, musicians, and actors. Like Patrick, these people didn't fit in growing up, so they weren't afraid to spend their lives standing out. They stood on stage in costumes every night, larger than life!

Patrick wanted to help his new friends, so he designed costumes for them, and Patrick's friends exclaimed:

"Patrick, they're too vibrant!"
"They're too tight!"
"They're too much!"
"They're PERFECT!"

The theater at the most popular nightclub in Paris hired Patrick to make costumes. He sewed and sewed. He sewed so much his machine blew out the electricity in his apartment. But Patrick laughed and carried on as best he could.

With no machine he continued, hand sewing by candlelight.

Every week, the stage was filled with the biggest, wildest, most outrageous costumes Patrick could imagine.

And every night, the crowds shouted:
"Fantastique!"
"Magnifique!"
"Trés chic!"

Pretty soon, everyone in Paris knew the name Patrick Kelly. Not because his style fit in with everyone in fashion, but because he stood out!

All the places that had ignored Patrick before asked him to put on the most important show in any fashion designer's career—a runway show!

This was his chance to show the world what clothes could be.

Patrick knew what he wanted to do right away—a Sunday church fashion parade.

Patrick hired models of every color, shape, and size. When they walked out, they were having fun!

They wore:

- dresses covered with plastic dolls, hearts, bows, pinwheels, dice, and pearls
- a toy crocodile for a scarf!
- a fur coat made from teddy bears
- and of course, lots and lots of buttons

Mama was right. The audience couldn't help but smile.

PATRICK KELLY
you

After the show, as cameras snapped Patrick's photo, magazine reporters asked him if his clothes had a message.

Patrick knew that all his family and friends who supported him, all the dancers and performers who had grown up feeling different like he had, would read the interview. To them he said "you're beautiful just the way you are."

Then, the reporters asked Patrick "why did you become a designer?"

And Patrick knew his words would appear in those magazines like the ones on Mama's porch. So to Mama, everyone he loved growing up, and shoppers everywhere, he said . . .

"I want my clothes to make you

SMILE."

PARIS

Patrick Kelly (1954–1990)

Patrick Leroy Kelly was one of the most important and influential fashion designers of the twentieth century. He was certainly the most fun.

Kelly was born on September 24, 1954, in the small, racially segregated city of Vicksburg, Mississippi. He was raised by his grandmother, Ethel Rainey, a caterer and domestic worker who cleaned the homes of wealthy White families in Vicksburg, and by his mother, Letha Kelly, a home economics teacher.

After graduating from high school in 1972, Kelly briefly attended Jackson State University, an HBCU (Historically Black Colleges and Universities). But he soon relocated to Atlanta, where he quickly became one of the city's most sought-after designers.

In 1978, he moved to New York City to study fashion design at the world-famous Parsons School of Design. In New York City, Kelly struggled financially, and as an extroverted, Black, gay Southerner dressed in his signature overalls, sneakers, and red bandannas or baseball hats, he found it difficult to be accepted by the snobbish American fashion establishment. By 1980, he had run out of money and was contemplating moving back home when his friend, supermodel Pat Cleveland, bought him a plane ticket to Paris and encouraged him to try his luck there. So he headed to the fashion capital of the world with the intent to break into the ultra-exclusive French fashion industry.

In Paris, Kelly's unique personal style and fashion designs were eventually embraced. In 1985—with the support of his life and business partner, Bjorn Amelan—Kelly established one of the hottest fashion labels of the 1980s, *Patrick Kelly*. His clothes were worn by a who's who of the world's most glamourous women, including "The Dianas" (that is, singer Diana Ross and Diana, Princess of Wales), film legends Cicely Tyson and Bette Davis, and pop stars Grace Jones and Madonna. His designs were featured in leading fashion publications including *Vogue*, *Elle*, *Harper's Bazaar*, *Ebony*, *Essence*, *Cosmopolitan*, and *Seventeen* magazine, to name only a few. He was also featured in profiles in some of the most widely read and respected newspapers including the *New York Times*, the *Washington Post*, and the *Los Angeles Times*.

Creating a unique style that, to some, was controversial for highlighting painful histories of racism in America and internationally, Kelly linked those histories to the everyday beauty and style of the South's Black poor and working classes, with the joy and glamour of Black pop icons, and his love of nightlife, visual art, and theater.

Kelly made history in 1988 when he became the first American invited to become a member of the exclusive century-old council that governs the French fashion industry, the Chambre Syndicale du Prêt-à-Porter des Couturiers et des Créateurs de Mode. This is considered by many to be the pinnacle of success in the world of high fashion.

Sadly, at the height of his success, Kelly became very ill. On January 1, 1990, he died at age thirty-five due to health complications from the auto-immune disease known as AIDS. His company closed its doors almost immediately after his death. Though Kelly's life and seat atop the world of fashion were far too brief, in his death he has remained a fashion icon and source of inspiration and folk hero for many of today's most successful fashion designers and creatives.

Author's Note

I first learned about Patrick Kelly in a television news report when I was eight years old. While his photograph was shown, the journalist talked about this man from Mississippi who had become a successful fashion designer in Paris. By then I was already enamored with fashion and style. My interest began as a seed planted while seeing my grandparents, mother, and her siblings take such joy in the simple pleasures of selecting clothes for every occasion: work, church, parties, or just a short walk to the grocery store. Like Patrick, to me fashion seemed like magic. The clothes made my own family of very limited financial resources go happily about their day despite whatever challenges they faced. Dressing well illuminated the beauty already inside them. But the day I first saw Patrick was like no other.

Before that news segment, I had not seen another Black fashion designer in print or television news. I was completely inspired. Though I knew nothing about Patrick, his big grin, denim overalls covered with buttons, and bashfulness led me to imagine that we were somehow kindred. I later learned that Patrick, like me, had grown up as a quirky and creative Black queer kid encouraged to pursue his greatest, grandest dreams. Like me, he also was empowered by women in his life—especially his grandmother—to have faith and never give up on himself or the inherent goodness in others. For Patrick, his dream was about a life creating beautiful and fun clothes for everyone, no matter their background. He believed clothes, like the people he dressed, had personalities and conveyed feelings. Patrick called his designs "happy clothes" because he intended for every garment to put a smile on the face of its wearer and anyone who saw them throughout their day. My dream was to tell the stories of people like Patrick so that their lives will never be forgotten, and their work will always encourage us. So in some ways I have been writing *Clothes to Make You Smile* since age eight. My heart and mind were certainly made up then to know more about this unique, creative, joyful, stylish man from Vicksburg, Mississippi, and to share all I learned about him with others.

My journey to know more about Patrick and to tell his story has taken me many places, from his hometown to Paris. I started my research about him not where he was born but at his final resting place: the tomb where he is buried at Père Lachaise cemetery in Paris. There, engraved beneath his name on a tombstone, is an epitaph: "NOTHING IS IMPOSSIBLE"—words Patrick repeated throughout his life to inspire himself to keep going when it seemed his dreams to make it in the world of fashion might never come true. I hope that this book about Patrick's life and creations will always be there when you—or someone you know—needs the reminder that our dreams are achievable, that standing out is a superpower, that creating and sharing things that bring more joy to a sometimes sad, scary world is a choice we can make every day, and most of all, that Patrick Kelly loves you.

Select Bibliography

Books

Pritchard, E. "Race WERK: Williwear and Patrick Kelly Paris." In *Black Designers in American Fashion*, edited by Elizabeth Way. Bloomsbury Publishing, 2021.

Pritchard, E. "Sex, Sexuality, and Signifying: Patrick Kelly's Queer Enterprise." In *Patrick Kelly: Runway of Love*, edited by Laura L. Camerlengo. Yale University Press, 2021.

Articles

Pritchard, E. "Black Supernovas: Black Gay Fashion Designers as Critical Intellectual Resource for Contemporary Black Fashion Studies." *International Journal of Fashion Studies* 4, no. 1 (2017): 107–110.

Pritchard, E. "Overalls: On Identity and Aspiration from Patrick Kelly's Fashion to Hip Hop." *The Funambulist*, January–February 2018.

Pritchard, E. "Tapestry: Generations and Geographies of Black Fashion Genius." *Black Fashion Fair* 0 (2022): 10–17.

Lectures/Interviews

Calahan, April, and Cassidy Zachary, hosts. *Dressed: The History of Fashion.* "Patrick Kelly, an Interview with Eric Darnell Pritchard." Dressed Media, aired September 24, 2019. Podcast, 57 min. www.iheart.com/podcast/105-dressed-the-history-of-fas-29000690/episode/patrick-kelly-an-interview-with-dr-49618187.

Kelly, Patrick. "Faces and Places in Fashion: Patrick Kelly." Archive on Demand, recorded on April 24, 1989. Video, 1 hr., 2 min. www.youtube.com/watch?v=-_gMSO_KjRc.

Miller, Monica, and E. Pritchard. "Symposium | Dr. Monica Miller and Eric Darnell Pritchard in conversation about Patrick Kelly." The Museum at FIT, August 14, 2017. Video, 44 min. www.youtube.com/watch?v=ve8dpb73hCc.

Film

Natara Harper, Rashidi, dir. *Patrick Kelly: The American in Paris*. Fine Arts Museums of San Francisco, 2021. www.youtube.com/watch?v=u59WAjIdqfM.

Notes

Page 39: "I design for all kinds of women. My message is you're beautiful just the way you are." —Patrick Kelly, from Bonnie Johnson, "In Paris, His Slinky Dresses Have Made Mississippi-Born Designer Patrick Kelly the New King of Cling," *People*, June 15, 1987.

Page 40: "I want my clothes to make you smile!" —Patrick Kelly, from Nina Hyde, "From Pauper to the Prints of Paris," *The Washington Post*, November 9, 1986, G1.